Jessie Anand Productions in association with
Neil McPherson for the Finborough Theatre
presents

The world premiere

PENNYROYAL
by Lucy Roslyn

First performance at the Finborough Theatre, London,
on Tuesday 12 July 2022.

PENNYROYAL

by Lucy Roslyn

Cast in order of speaking

CHRISTINE	**Lucy Roslyn**
DAPHNE	**Madison Clare**

The approximate running time is seventy-five minutes. There will be no interval.

Director	**Josh Roche**
Set and Costume Designer	**Sophie Thomas**
Lighting Designer	**Cheng Keng**
Composer and Sound Designer	**Hugh Sheehan**
Associate Set and Costume Designer	**Kit Hinchcliffe**
Producer	**Jessie Anand**
Stage Manager	**Kit Fowler**

PLEASE BE CONSIDERATE OF OTHERS AND WEAR A FACE COVERING FULLY COVERING YOUR MOUTH AND NOSE FOR THE DURATION OF THE PERFORMANCE.

Please see front of house notices or ask an usher for an exact running time. Please turn your mobile phones off – the light they emit can also be distracting.

Our patrons are respectfully reminded that, in this intimate theatre, any noise such as the rustling of programmes, food packaging or talking may distract the actors and your fellow audience members. We regret there is no admittance or re-admittance to the auditorium whilst the performance is in progress.

Lucy Roslyn | Christine

Productions at the Finborough Theatre include *A Third*.

Trained at Drama Studio London.

Playwriting and Performing includes *Orlando* (VAULT Festival and Edinburgh Fringe); *Showmanship* (Edinburgh Fringe, Brighton Fringe, Theatre503 and Assembly Gardens, Coventry); *Goody* (Edinburgh Fringe and Greenwich Theatre) and *The State vs. John Hayes* (Edinburgh Fringe, Theatre Royal Bath, The Lowry, King's Head Theatre and Old Stone House, Brooklyn).

Performing includes *Life and Death of a Journalist* (VAULT Festival), *Mr Happiness* and *The Water Engine* (The Old Vic Tunnels), *Chicken Shop* and *Crystal Springs* (Park Theatre), *She Ventures and He Wins* (Rose Playhouse) and *Money vs. Happiness* (Battersea Arts Centre).

Madison Clare | Daphne

Productions at the Finborough Theatre include *Masks and Faces* online.

Trained at London Academy of Music and Dramatic Art.

Theatre includes *Captain Corelli's Mandolin* (Harold Pinter Theatre and National Tour); *Bin Juice* (VAULT Festival); *Plastic* (Old Red Lion Theatre) and *War Whores* (Courtyard Theatre).

Television includes *Semi-Detached*, *Grantchester*, *Holby City* and *Jesus: His Life*.

Josh Roche | Director

Productions at the Finborough Theatre include *Magnificence* and *A Third*.

Theatre includes the JMK Award winning *My Name is Rachel Corrie* (Young Vic); *No Particular Order* (Theatre503); *Home* (Chichester Festival Theatre); *Orlando* (VAULT Festival and Pleasance Edinburgh); *Resurrecting Bobby Awl* (Summerhall Edinburgh, BBC Arts and Avalon); *Radio* (Arcola Theatre and Audible); *Plastic* (Old Red Lion Theatre and Mercury Theatre, Colchester); *(I Feel Fine)* (VAULT Festival and New Diorama Theatre) and *Winky* (Underbelly Edinburgh and Soho Theatre).

Associate Direction includes David Haig's *Pressure* (Park Theatre, Ambassadors Theatre and National Tour).

Assistant Direction includes *The Taming of the Shrew* (Shakespeare's Globe); *Eternal Love* (English Touring Theatre); *Death of a Salesman* (Royal Shakespeare Company and Noël Coward Theatre); *Doctor Faustus* and *The Alchemist* (Royal Shakespeare Company and Barbican Theatre) and *Farinelli and the King* (Duke of York's Theatre).

Josh is the co-founder of the OpenHire campaign. He is also a reader for Sonia Friedman Productions and former Literary Associate at Soho Theatre.

Sophie Thomas | Set and Costume Designer

Trained at Oxford Brookes University and Royal Welsh College of Music and Drama.

Theatre includes *Home* (Chichester Festival Theatre); *Radio* (Arcola Theatre and Audible); *Orlando* (VAULT Festival and Pleasance Edinburgh); *Resurrecting Bobby Awl* (Summerhall Edinburgh, BBC Arts and Avalon); *Plastic* (Old Red Lion Theatre and Mercury Theatre, Colchester); *My Name is Rachel Corrie* (Young Vic); *Herons* and *The Imaginary Misogynist* (Guildhall School of Music and Drama); *The Slave* (Tristan Bates Theatre) and *Henry V* (Cambridge Arts Theatre).

Film includes *Carnage: Swallowing the Past*, *Never Land*, *New Gods*, *Ringo*, *The Listener* and *And Then I Was French*.

Sophie was Resident Assistant Designer at the Royal Shakespeare Company 2015-16.

Cheng Keng | Lighting Designer

Trained at National Taiwan University of Art and Royal Central School of Speech and Drama.

Theatre includes *Birdie and the Animal Kingdom* (Harrow Arts Centre); *Beauty and the 7 Beasts* (Brixton Jamm); *Borders* (Drayton Arms Theatre); *7homes* (online exhibition); *Extremist* (Royal Central School of Speech and Drama); *@ iContact: Mirror Talk* (International Tour); *Blue Island 99* (International Dublin Gay Theatre Festival and Sydney Fringe Festival) and *Hello World* (NTT, Taiwan).

Hugh Sheehan | Composer and Sound Designer

Productions at the Finborough Theatre include *Magnificence*.

Trained at Royal Welsh College

of Music and Drama and Sibelius Academy.

Theatre includes *The 4th Country* (Park Theatre); *The Hole* (Old Rep Theatre, Birmingham); *Pomona* (Gate Theatre and Richard Burton Theatre, Royal Welsh College) and *Beasts and Beauties* (Richard Burton Theatre, Royal Welsh College).

In 2019, Hugh was commissioned by BBC Arts and Arts Council England to make an audio work entitled *Lost Time* for their New Creatives series.

Kit Hinchcliffe | Associate Set and Costume Designer
Trained at Central St Martins College of Art and Design.

Theatre, Dance and Opera includes *Mapping Gender* (BALTIC Centre for Contemporary Art and The Place); *La bohème* (King's Head Theatre); *Boys* (Barbican Theatre); *Festen* (Corbett Theatre, East 15); *Tender Napalm* (King's Head Theatre); *Well Lit* (The Place and Dansstationen Malmö); *Ali and Dalia* and *Moonfleece* (Pleasance London); *Pebbles* (Katzpace); *Heroes* (Bridge House Theatre) and *Beetles from the West* (Hope Theatre).

Kit is a key member of the team at Architecture Social Club where she works as a designer/fabricator, and is also co-artistic director of Lidless Theatre.

Jessie Anand | Producer
Jessie is a producer and general manager working across theatre and opera.

Theatre as Producer includes *The Silver Bell* (King's Head Theatre, International Dublin Gay Theatre Festival and forthcoming Edinburgh Fringe run); *Yellowfin* (Southwark Playhouse), *MAGDALENE* (Arcola Theatre); *Blue Thunder* (VAULT Festival) and *Orlando* (VAULT Festival and Pleasance Edinburgh).

Assistant and Associate Producer credits include *The Language of Kindness* (Warwick Arts Centre, Assembly Hall Theatre Tunbridge Wells and Shoreditch Town Hall) and *Licensed To Ill* (Latitude Festival and Southwark Playhouse).

Opera includes *Liturgie* and *Helena* (Tête à Tête), *Collision* and *Treemonisha* (Arcola Theatre); *The Boatswain's Mate* (Arcola Theatre and forthcoming National Tour) and *Cabildo* (Arcola Theatre and Wilton's Music Hall).

Opera as Assistant or Associate Producer includes *La bohème* (King's Head Theatre) and *Found and Lost* (Corinthia Hotel, London).

Jessie is supported by Stage One, and has previously worked for the National Theatre, The Corner Shop PR and Wayward Productions.

Kit Fowler | Stage Manager
Trained at London Academy of Music and Dramatic Art.

Theatre includes *Jerusalem*, *Ivanov*, *Aida*, *Funny Girl*, *Sweet Charity* (ADC Theatre, Cambridge); *Much Ado About Nothing* (US Tour); *Six Characters in Search of an Author* (Edinburgh Fringe); *Three Sisters* (LAMDA); *Henry V* (Cambridge Arts Theatre); *Arden Creatures* (Cockpit Theatre) and *Can't Stand Up For Falling Down* (Bedford Theatre).

Production Acknowledgements

Graphic Design	**Katie Allen**
Trailer Design	**Katie Edwards**
Rehearsal Photography	**Cam Harle**
Production Photography	**Helen Murray**
PR	**Kevin Wilson**
Workshop Leader	**Alice McCabe**
Captioning	**Claire Hill**

We would like to thank the following for advising us about the content of the play: Kathy Abernethy, former Chair of the British Menopause Society; Amy Bennie, Chair of Daisy Network; Bianka Kuhn and Fiona Thompson-Kuhn; Fiona Lacey.

Special thanks go to Asha Reid for performing as Daphne throughout the development of the piece.

Supported using public funding by
**ARTS COUNCIL
ENGLAND**

This production is supported by Arts Council England, New Diorama Theatre, the Bryan Guinness Charitable Trust, Felix Danczak, Julian Danczak, Georgina Harding and a number of other individuals.

jessie
anand

Jessie Anand Productions makes theatre and opera that is fresh and playful. Since it was founded in 2018, it has premiered four new plays: the OffWestEnd Award winning *Yellowfin* by Marek Horn (Southwark Playhouse), *MAGDALENE* by Mary Galloway (Arcola Theatre), *Orlando* by Lucy Roslyn (VAULT Festival and Edinburgh Fringe) and the site-specific piece *Blue Thunder*, which played a sold-out run at VAULT Festival in 2019 and has since been adapted for BBC Radio 4.

The company's opera work includes *Cabildo* (Wilton's Music Hall and Arcola Theatre) and a digital production of *The Telephone* in partnership with Guildhall School of Music and Drama.

Projects currently in development include a new musical, *The Wife of Michael Cleary*, and a new witch play for today inspired by *The Late Lancashire Witches* and *The Witch of Edmonton*.

Jessie Anand Productions is supported by Stage One.

FINBOROUGH THEATRE

'Probably the most influential fringe theatre in the world.'
Time Out

'Not just a theatre, but a miracle.'
Metro

'The mighty little Finborough which, under Neil McPherson,
continues to offer a mixture of neglected classics and new
writing in a cannily curated mix.'
Lyn Gardner, *The Stage*

'The tiny but mighty Finborough'
Ben Brantley, *The New York Times*

Founded in 1980, the multi-award-winning Finborough Theatre
presents plays and music theatre, concentrated exclusively on
vibrant new writing and unique rediscoveries from the 19th and
20th centuries, both in our 154 year old home and online through
our #FinboroughFrontier digital initiative. Our programme is
unique – we never present work that has been seen anywhere in
London during the last 25 years. Behind the scenes, we continue to
discover and develop a new generation of theatre makers.

www.finboroughtheatre.co.uk

FINBOROUGH THEATRE

The Finborough Theatre is a member of the Independent Theatre Council, the Society of Independent Theatres, Musical Theatre Network, The Friends of Brompton Cemetery, The Earl's Court Society, The Kensington Society, and supports #time4change's Mental Health Charter

The Finborough Theatre receives no regular funding from the Royal Borough of Kensington and Chelsea.

Mailing
Email admin@finboroughtheatre.co.uk or give your details to our Box Office staff to join our free email list.

Playscripts
Many of the Finborough Theatre's plays have been published and are on sale from our website.

Electricity
The Finborough Theatre has a 100% sustainable electricity supply.

Local History
The Finborough Theatre's local history website is online at
www.earlscourtlocalhistory.co.uk

On Social Media
The Finborough Theatre is on Facebook, Twitter, Instagram, YouTube and TikTok.

Friends
The Finborough Theatre is a registered charity. We receive no public funding, and rely solely on the support of our audiences. Please do consider supporting us by becoming a member of our Friends of the Finborough Theatre scheme. There are four categories of Friends, each offering a wide range of benefits.

Richard Tauber Friends
David and Melanie Alpers. James Baer. David Barnes. Mike Bartlett. Kate Beswick. Simon Bolland. Malcolm Cammack. James Carroll. Denis Crapnell. Michael Diamond. Richard Dyer. Catrin Evans. Deirdre Feehan. Jeff Fergus. Anne Foster. Patrick Foster. Julia Gallop. Nancy Goldring. David Grier. Judith Gunton. David Hammond. Mary Hickson. Christine Hoenigs. Laurence Humphreys-Davies. Damien Hyland. Richard Jackson. Paul and Lindsay Kennedy. Martin and Wendy Kramer. Alex Laird. Georgina and Dale Lang. John Lawson. Emilia Leese. Frederick Lock. Rebecca Maltby. Kathryn McDowall. Ghazell Mitchell. Graham Orpwood. Frederick Pyne. Maroussia Richardson. Annette Riddle. Elaine and Fred Rizzo. Chris Robinson. L Schulz. John Shea. Brian Smith. James Stitt. Janet Swirski. Caroline Thompson. Jan Topham. Lavinia Webb. Joan Weingarten and Bob Donnalley. John Wilkes. Steven Williams. Laura Winningham. Jonathan Woods. Sylvia Young.

William Terriss Friends
Patrick Foster. Janet and Leo Liebster. Ros and Alan Haigh.

Adelaide Neilson Friends
Charles Glanville. Philip G Hooker.

PENNYROYAL

Lucy Roslyn

Author's Note
Lucy Roslyn

> 'Here they were at last face to face with the problem
> which, through all the years of silence and evasiveness,
> had lain as close to the surface as a corpse too hastily
> buried.' *The Old Maid*, Edith Wharton

Just before the Covid pandemic hit, Josh Roche introduced me
to the striking 1922 novella *The Old Maid*. It's about the close
relationship between two women becoming taut and knotted in
the face of family values and societal expectations. It showed
complicated, loving, fuming, forgiving women and the drawn-
out repercussions of a life lived bending to the rules. There's an
image in their minds of the people they thought they would be,
and the brittle acceptance of the people they've become.

It is ugly, and beautiful, and relatable in many ways.

I have a sister and I'm extremely lucky to be very close to her.
She is a writer herself (an extraordinary one). During lockdown
I spoke with her a few times about our dreams and aspirations.
About not losing hope in the things we had set out to do. After
ten years of trying to find a footing for my work, at the closing
of the theatres I felt the gig was, perhaps, finally up. *Pennyroyal*
is about sisterhood. Enduring love. The rocky, unplanned way
that life works out. The opportunities, if you seek them, to find
your way back to people. I hope it will resonate with others, just
as Edith Wharton's story resonated with me.

I am indebted to the people I spoke to and resources I read about
Premature Ovarian Insufficiency. There's a running theme of
frustration that women's health is kept in the shadows. How
you are supposed to stagger, quietly, from one stage of life into
another. That these stages can be the curveball that shakes the
very image of yourself and the things you hope for. It is a many
layered topic and I hope I have done it some justice. Overall this

is a story of a relationship. A joyous one, I feel. Two magnets, trying to get back to each other. It is with heartfelt thanks to the *Pennyroyal* team that we have made it this far.

To Hugh, Sophie and Cheng for their incredible artistry. To Kit for making our rehearsals so smooth and positive.

To Jessie, for steering this ship with such elegance and energy. To Madison, 'my Daphne'. To Nick Hern Books for their support as we fought to get this play on. To Asha for her help on the journey.

To Josh, you've been my champion since I wrote my first play in 2012. I already look forward to our next thing.
To David of the NDT. This is the second time you have stepped up for us.
To the Finborough Theatre, for welcoming us in.
To my family, forever in my corner.
To Pip. My cat. You're gorgeous.
To Gloria Estefan, 'Anything for You' is a perfect song.
And to Jamie Firth of BoonDog Theatre, for your creativity and help as we read through draft after draft late into the night. Thank you for holding the umbrella.

4

Characters

DAPHNE (DAFF), *female, Christine's sister*
CHRISTINE, *female, Daphne's sister*

Note on the Text

/ indicates overlapping lines
– indicates interruption
[ ] indicates intended but unspoken dialogue

This text went to press before the end of rehearsals and so may differ slightly from the play as performed.

Christmas Eve in a family home. The space is nineties nostalgic.

There is a feeling of dark, blustery wilderness outside.

DAFF, *in a world of her own, is applying Christmas decorations on stage.*

CHRIS *watches from a seat in the audience, she has a bottle and two glasses. She is already drinking.*

CHRIS. When I think about Daphne this is what I picture.

She looks round to the audience.

Sorry I should say, I'm part of this. I am a part of this.

I just wanted to see what she looked like from here.

She gestures DAFF, *oblivious on stage.*

This is Daphne.

Daphne always does the decorations, like… this is her Christmas ritual. Mum's Christmas ritual is that she always makes lasagne. And my Christmas ritual is… I dress up the dog. Yep… that's my thing. The dog used to be an Elvis, but we lost the wig, so now the dog's Elton John (*She chuckles at the memory.*)

We watch *It's a Wonderful Life*. And every year it's like… (*Hand to heart.*) 'I want to live!' I just… love it.

She focuses on DAFF *decorating the tree.*

It was a box office flop when it first came out. People didn't know quite what they were looking at, so they didn't like it. (*As Jimmy Stewart.*) 'Can you believe that? They didn't like it, can you believe it! See, if you'd seen the film you'd know – Jimmy Stewart!'

Anyway…

She gazes at DAFF *on stage, derailed.*

When I think about Daff – this is how I see her.

She used to decorate the tree with Dad.

She takes a drink of wine and watches her sister decorate.

This is her at nineteen. So that would make me... twenty-six? I'll be twenty-six. I remember I walked in and I offered her a drink.

Without missing a beat, DAFF *speaks out to* CHRIS *in the audience.*

DAFF. No you didn't.

CHRIS. Uh, yes I did I said 'Hey Daff, are you home? Do you want a drink?'

DAFF. No, you just said 'Hey Daff'.

CHRIS. No, I said 'Hey Daff, you home?', 'Yeah', 'Want a drink?' and then I asked where Bumble was.

DAFF. That's not what you said.

CHRIS. It is.

   DAFF, *onstage, stops decorating and stares directly out at* CHRIS. *They hesitate.*

DAFF. I'm running out of decorations if you want to / think any quicker –

   CHRIS *immediately interrupts, abruptly starting the play.*

CHRIS. / – Hey Daff, you home?!

DAFF (*immediately*). Yeah?

CHRIS. Want a drink? Where's Bumble?

   A dog barks offstage – Bumble.

DAFF. Bumble's in / the garden with Mum.

CHRIS. / the garden with Mum.

DAFF. Fuck you.

   CHRIS *holds out a glass.* DAFF *reluctantly walks over to take it. The play begins.*

Home

The sisters settle under the tree with drinks. Something is wrong with DAPHNE.

DAFF. I didn't know you'd be back so soon. Are you back?

CHRIS. I am back.

DAFF. Long journey.

CHRIS. Ah, don't worry about it.

> CHRIS *watches* DAFF *lovingly.*

> You want to talk about it?

> DAFF *shakes her head – no.*

DAFF. Mum's making lasagne tonight.

CHRIS. Excellent.

> CHRIS *smiles kindly at* DAFF. DAFF *tries to look strong, something is clearly wrong.* CHRIS *fiddles with some of the crappier homemade decorations.*

> You've done a nice job of this. Good to see some of the classics are out. Look at that, yoghurt pot Santa… never quite made it into the bin did he? And we can't bin him now!

DAFF (*looks lost*). No…

CHRIS. Have you moved home properly then? What about the scholarship?

> DAFF *laughs mirthlessly and shakes her head.*

> What about Ian?

DAFF (*deflecting*). I saw Mum walking round the garden last night. She was standing in her nightgown, so I went out in my pyjamas. She says she thinks better outside.

CHRIS. Did you talk?

DAFF. She talked about motherhood… I broke it off with Ian.

Beat. DAFF *chooses her words carefully*.

I am under a cloud, Chris.

CHRIS. I'll come under it with you then.

I'll hold the umbrella.

Beat.

Did you love him?

DAFF *doesn't know*.

Did you give him a chance?

DAFF. To what?

CHRIS. He might not want kids.

DAFF. He proposed.

CHRIS. Okay…! Okay?

DAFF. I don't think he knows what he's doing. I mean, we're on the same course but we don't really know each other that well.

CHRIS. Okay?

DAFF. He'll lose his hair when he's older. He's a bald man, he just doesn't know it yet.

CHRIS. Right.

DAFF. He's a romantic.

CHRIS. Well what is he, nineteen? Twenty?

DAFF. Eighteen.

CHRIS. 'kay.

DAFF. He's not thinking ahead.

CHRIS. Is this the guy I met at Halloween? Dressed like a rubber glove?

DAFF. He was a prawn. We were both prawns. He says he sees me.

CHRIS (*unimpressed*). Right.

DAFF. He helped me make my costume. And then he…
(*Cheeky.*) he helped me take it off. All the little legs…

DAFF *gestures suggestively, the opening of her many prawn legs, like many bras coming off.* CHRIS *looks repulsed.*

What?

CHRIS. What?

DAFF. You're frowning

CHRIS. Yeah. Is this a… 'pants off' story? Your pants come
off?

DAFF. Yeah.

CHRIS (*frowning, repulsed*). Okay.

DAFF. You look like De Niro

CHRIS. Do I? (*Leaning into it for laughs. A full blown Robert
De Niro impression.*) 'Do I? I do hope this is an explicit
story where your pants, they come right off. I love to feel
awkward.'

DAFF (*joining in. A De Niro impression*). 'No, you got to wag
the finger.'

CHRIS. 'Wag that finger. That's De Niro, there he is.'

DAFF. 'There he is!'

CHRIS. 'There he is! He loves an awkward story, you know
that.'

DAFF. 'He does, yes he does!'

They wag their fingers at each other.

The flicker of playfulness passes, DAFF's *smile fades.*

CHRIS. Daff?

DAFF. He says he doesn't want kids, but he's lying.

CHRIS. Do you want kids?

DAFF. I don't think it matters at this point.

CHRIS. Did the doctors say? Is that what / the doctors –

DAFF. / Chris…

There's no point discussing it.

CHRIS. Premature Ovarian… / Failure?

DAFF. / Insufficiency.

CHRIS. Insufficiency.

DAFF. They're trying not to say 'menopause' but that's the basic… that's the gist.

CHRIS. Right… (*Beat.*) Did you want kids?

DAFF (*snaps*). Fucking hell! Sorry, I'm sorry –

CHRIS. Don't be sorry.

DAFF. I just – I don't know. I didn't think about it Chris. I didn't think about it. And now… I think about – yeah, I think about them sitting next to me. I think about them running out of school and making friends. I think about Mum.

CHRIS. What does she say?

DAFF. She says I would have made a wonderful mother.

Beat.

CHRIS. Well, that's not very helpful.

DAFF. She says we both would.

CHRIS *looks surprised.*

You ever think about it?

CHRIS. I'll be honest with you Daff, I think I thought… No. I think 'No.'

DAFF. Did you talk to Mum about it?

CHRIS. I did.

DAFF. You talk about me?

CHRIS *nods.*

CHRIS. So what makes you think he's lying?

DAFF. I don't know. Seems like the nice thing to do, to lie.

CHRIS. Have you told anybody else?

DAFF. I told Aubrey.

CHRIS. Eurgh.

DAFF (*mildly amused*). You don't like her.

CHRIS. I've never liked her.

DAFF. Why not?!

CHRIS. She flirts with me.

DAFF. She's my oldest friend.

CHRIS. Yep.

DAFF. She flirts with you? Shall I tell her you've got a
boyfriend?

CHRIS. I think –

DAFF. – Do you have a boyfriend? Are you not seeing
someone?

CHRIS. I think – No I'm… no. Not seeing anyone – I just
think… (*Elusive*.) I think that's just the kind of person
Aubrey is.

Beat.

DAFF. Do you think she's hot?

CHRIS. No. I mean, she is attractive in a children's tv presenter,
kind of… zero sex-appeal kind of a way. Well, that's not
fair. Y'know what it is? She's the kind of person who would
drops hints about her sex life, know what I mean? Fly some
facts in under the radar.

DAFF *grins*.

DAFF. You don't like her.

CHRIS. She's insecure and I think you should be wary of
insecure people.

DAFF. When Aubrey and I were kids we used to fantasise about raising our children together. We used to joke that we wouldn't recognise whose kids belonged to who.

CHRIS. I think you would recognise.

DAFF (*stepping carefully*). I think I told her because, when it comes to the crunch... she's a good friend. So I think I told her because I knew she would offer... to help.

CHRIS. To help?

DAFF. To donate.

A tense pause. What is the correct response?

CHRIS. Don't.

DAFF. What?

CHRIS. Eggs?

DAFF. Yes.

CHRIS. Don't.

DAFF. I don't think you / realise what it would mean –

CHRIS. / Don't! Daff. Oh my God – Aubrey's eggs. With what... with Ian? Do you want bald children with zero sex-appeal? I mean honestly, c'mon...

DAFF (*heated*). I hadn't accepted yet I'm just / telling you!

CHRIS. / Well don't. Be friends with her but don't do that. It doesn't matter how separate someone thinks / they can be –

DAFF. / They're just eggs.

CHRIS. Yeah, but there's dominant genes there, Daff.

DAFF. She wouldn't be the one raising them.

CHRIS. No, no I get that, I get that. I'm just thinking, like... in what world would she... let go.

Like, in what world is she not hovering over them, or you, know what I mean?

DAFF. I'm not asking your advice!

CHRIS. I think you are asking my advice about Aubrey, and I have doubts, man.

DAFF. As a donor?

CHRIS. As a person, who lives on the earth. 'Donor' – Daff, fucking hell. Listen, what did she go as for Halloween?

DAFF. Is this your test?

CHRIS. You went as a glove –

DAFF. – I was a prawn -

CHRIS. – A prawn, okay and she was a...?

DAFF. Cat.

CHRIS. What kind of cat?

DAFF. A / sexy cat.

CHRIS. / Sexy cat. (*She gestures: There it is.*)

DAFF. You know, that was the last time – that halloween... I knew exactly who I was.

They take a breath and deflect. CHRIS *looks about the house.*

CHRIS. I love coming home. I sometimes think what I'd do if it was mine. Greenhouse. Workshop in the garage. Turn my room into a study.

DAFF. Would you leave the clouds?

CHRIS. I'd paint more clouds Daff! To go with the ones I painted when I was fifteen. I'd expand my shrine for Gloria Estefan.

DAFF. What would you do with my room?

She escapes into a daydream.

Where would I be, I'd be dancing. In New York. I'd be a choreographer.

CHRIS. Oh yeah?

DAFF. Yeah. I'd wear shades in the studio. Drink martini out of a flask. People would say 'I'm worried about her, she's brilliant.' I'd be Bob Fosse, basically! I'm tired all the time.

DAFF *shrugs, hopeless*.

CHRIS. If you want to drink martinis with me I'll get my shades out the car?

DAFF. I wanted to be more.

CHRIS (*forcefully*). You are more.

DAFF (*swallowing her grief*). So, what would you do with my room?

CHRIS. I'd seal it off like a tomb. Throw some sage in, brick it up.

DAFF. Sounds about right.

CHRIS. I'd plant some flowers in it, Daff.

DAFF (*sadly*). Thank you. Did Mum tell you what she said to me?

CHRIS. She said she'd remortgage the house and help you out which… Right. Is that what – is this what it's for?

DAFF. If I had a donor. (*She nods.*) It would be just like IVF. So I could carry a baby, it just – it wouldn't be mine.

CHRIS. It would be Aubrey's.

DAFF (*laughs it off*). They wouldn't be Aubrey's.

CHRIS (*she touches her own ear*). No 'crinkle ear' then.

DAFF (*a sad laugh*). No, no famous 'crinkle ear'.

CHRIS. Lets see?

DAFF *shows* CHRIS *her ear.* CHRIS *smiles*.

There it is.

DAFF. When you talked with Mum…?

CHRIS. She told me about the mortgage but, I don't know – she doesn't give much away.

DAFF (*sharply*). Did she ask you this?

CHRIS. No! No.

DAFF. Cause I know we always joke (*Mocking the family catchphrase*.) 'Oh, Chris'll do it!'

CHRIS (*laughing it off*). No no no. She just said 'Come home'.

DAFF. You talk?

CHRIS. We talk well on the phone but then… I don't know, I think she forgets how much I look like Dad. What does Mum think of Aubrey?

DAFF. I haven't told her that.

CHRIS (*the horror*). Grandmother to Aubrey's children.

DAFF (*stern*). They wouldn't be Aubrey's.

CHRIS. Aubrey doesn't get on well with her own mother does she?

DAFF. I think she's a difficult woman.

CHRIS. Which one?

DAFF *laughs, tired. She gives off a slightly fractured, scattershot vibe in an attempt to avoid her feelings.*

I'm so sorry Daff.

DAFF. I'll be doing hormone replacement therapy for the rest of my life. And if you don't do it your bones dry up. And your brain dries up. Your womb crumbles down your trouser leg.

CHRIS. Daff –

DAFF. You'll be coming after me with a dustpan and brush (*She laughs, desperate. Divert.*) Do you want to watch *It's a Wonderful Life* this evening?

CHRIS. Absolutely.

DAFF. Do you think in another version of the film he stands on the bridge… and then he jumps?

DAFF's mask slips completely, she looks shell shocked, fearful.

CHRIS reaches out with concern and takes DAFF's hand.

DAFF plays with the sleeve absently.

(*Quietly.*) I like your jumper.

At this CHRIS shuffles over to sit beside her.

CHRIS raises the front of her jumper and brings it over DAFF, enveloping her completely like a kangaroo in a pouch.

She hugs the shape of DAFF. DAFF speaks from within.

I feel like everything mysterious about me has gone. Like I was a book with chapters and now.

I'm just a pamphlet.

CHRIS. Lift your arms up.

As DAFF raises her arms CHRIS shuffles the sleeves down onto her.

Eventually CHRIS ducks out, leaving DAFF wearing the jumper. DAFF smiles.

Y'know what I think?

DAFF. What?

CHRIS. I bought you a book about pickling and a pickling jar for Christmas, and now I can't help but feel that this gift is... suboptimal.

DAFF bursts out laughing.

I was watching a documentary about preserves –

DAFF (*sarcastically*). – You're really living, huh?

CHRIS. Oh fuck yeah. And the pickling – picklers – they just looked so satisfied. But as a gift... I don't know, man.

DAFF. I think it sounds nice. Preserving something. Do you think you'll stay for New Years?

CHRIS *nods*. DAFF *speaks, a hideous confession*.

We used to joke about menopause in biology class.

CHRIS (*brush it off*). Daff, we all did that!

DAFF (*frustration, with peaks of barely concealled rage*). Then
why didn't they make us take it seriously? Mrs Anderson
must have been fifty? Maybe fifty-five? She was probably in
menopause and she didn't think to bring it up? It's a biology
class, you know what I mean? She should have just said:
'Well, jokes on you.' But she didn't.

And we sat there like: (*Cocky teen*.) When menopause hits
we'll just go live in a hut in the woods, and grow a beard.
And the hut will be made from, fucking… flapjack.'

Cause that's who lives in the woods.

CHRIS. Bakers?

DAFF (*not playing*). Chris! Witches live in the wood. God, she
must have hated us, absolutely hated us… I would.

CHRIS. Daff –

DAFF. You know that giant rock in Australia?

CHRIS. Have you been googling?

DAFF. Yeah. There's a whole side of that rock dedicated to
childbirth. And Aboriginal women would give birth and the
rocks are like gaping, red. Like a cathedral. Women who died
in childbirth were treated like warriors.

Long thoughtful beat.

Did you know Mum buys lube?

CHRIS *tries to stay dignified*.

Don't laugh.

CHRIS. I'm not.

DAFF (*subdued, embarrassed*). Mum buys lubricant and she
doubled her order… for me.

CHRIS (*big breath*). I love you Daff.

DAFF. I was trying to read about it, anything that's not a
pamphlet.

Did you know that humans and a small number of whales
are the only mammals that go through the menopause? They
stop having kids, but they carry on. Beluga Whale. The
Narwhal... Then I read this story about a whale that was
singing at a different frequency so the other whales couldn't
hear it, it just... swam.

CHRIS. What frequency are you singing at?

DAFF *shrugs – lost.*

(*Sings a single high pitched note, like a howl.*)
Hoooooooooouuu!

Compelled, DAFF *matches the note exactly.*

DAFF. Hoooooooooouuu!

They howl quietly together.

CHRIS. Same. (*She grins.*)

DAFF. We sound like wolves. Are you back then d'you think?

CHRIS. I can be.

DAFF. I don't want to sing 'Auld Lang's Syne' this year.

CHRIS. Okay.

DAFF. It's the tune. I think it's sad.

For a moment DAFF *seems overcome.*

*The struggle to maintain a train of thought, the deep sadness
if she stops leaping from one thought to another. She gathers
herself.*

CHRIS. Well, we could sing... we could do a bit of Estefan? Or
we could sing Mum's favourite?!

Puzzled look from DAFF.

'Don't Worry Baby.'

DAFF. That's Mum's favourite?

CHRIS. It's The Beach Boys.

DAFF. I can't sing that high.

CHRIS.…We could sing your favourite.

DAFF (*she thinks for a moment*). I don't think I know what /
   that is?

   CHRIS *begins to sing the lead chorus from 'Babe' by Take
   That.*

   / It's not that! /

   Undetered, CHRIS *continues staggering through the song.*

   / That's not my favourite. /

   CHRIS *leaves the lyric hanging in the air, waiting for* DAFF
   to echo it. Compelled, DAFF *quietly joins in. The sisters
   finish the chorus together before petering out.* DAFF *tries to
   laugh but falls into despair. A silent moment.*

   DAFF *stares at* CHRIS *desperately.*

   Did Mum make you come here?

CHRIS. No.

DAFF. I didn't tell Mum to ask you.

CHRIS. I know.

DAFF. I didn't tell you about Aubrey's offer so you / would feel
   like you had…

CHRIS. / I know, I'm not trapped Daff. Well look, it's nearly
   Christmas, is there something you'd like?

DAFF. A pickling jar and a book about pickling.

CHRIS. I mean of course! But… is there something else?

   DAFF *covers her face with her hands – yes, there is
   something.*

   Is this you asking me?

DAFF *nods, face hidden.*

What if you change your mind?

DAFF. There's nothing like losing the option to make you
realise what you would have done.

The sisters stare at each other. DAFF *with hope,* CHRIS *with
conflict. Finally* CHRIS *nods.*

CHRIS. Well, let's do this then.

DAFF. Please be sure.

CHRIS. Are you kidding? I don't want to spend Christmas with
Aubrey's kids. I'd much rather spend it with your kids.

DAFF (*she samples the words, like nectar*). 'My kids.'

CHRIS. Daphne's kids.

DAFF *breaks into joyful tears.*

The sisters fall together laughing, they hug.

Conversation One

CHRIS *sits alone facing out.* DAFF *exits.* CHRIS *arranges
herself and speaks out.*

CHRIS. Right

She looks at the audience with mounting panic.

Oh no. D'you know what? No – (*Shouts offstage.*)

Daff? Daphne! Sorry, I've changed my – sorry…

Without hesitation DAFF *immediately reappears to sit beside
her.*

DAFF. Yep.

*They confer throughout, their speech overlapping at times.
They have become a tight unit, like kids.*

The sisters take the audience through the following years.

DAFF *is optimistic. They often derail each other.*

CHRIS. Right – so / this was our –

DAFF. / You don't want to do this by yourself?

CHRIS. No. This is way better. (*Together.*) So this was our year where we moved home. We lived together. Living with Mum. We're eating lasagne. We're walking Bumble.

DAFF. We're both taking hormones.

CHRIS. Doing hormones.

DAFF. That year I started my hormone therapy.

CHRIS. That year I started working at Hubbards Nursery. You quit your course.

DAFF. I did. Gave Ian his ring back.

(*Shamefully.*) I cut my bangs.

CHRIS. And what did I say?

BOTH. 'Sleep it off.'

CHRIS. Sleep it off. It'll pass.

DAFF. – You finished herbology.

CHRIS. My Horticulture course? *Horticulture.* Fucking nerd. But yeah, you just do it at home, y'know? You just learn what you were going to learn, but you learn it online in your room instead.

DAFF. Instead of what?

CHRIS. Instead of… learning it in another room where you're not there?

DAFF. You listen to *one* song, on a loop.

CHRIS. Yes I do, (*Proudly to the audience.*) and the song is 'Anything for You' by Gloria Estefan.

Because the song is – (*Chef's kiss: gorgeous.*)

DAFF (*a sudden memory*). I did your injections that year.

CHRIS....Yes, yes you did.

DAFF. Chris donated her eggs. (*Meaningful*.) That's what happened that year.

CHRIS. Yeah. Yeah I did... (*Deflect*.) I also grew West Indian gherkins that year.

DAFF. That year I grew weed.

CHRIS. Daphne!

DAFF. What?! It's medicinal. (DAFF *shakes her head to the audience – no it's not*.)

CHRIS. I remember standing in the garden and I was thinking 'Oh, the garden could be nice this...' (*Awkwardly*.) the hormones I was taking to produce... eggs, I mean – the bloating is... pretty heavy-going and... honestly, I thought I'd been giving off eggs like a salmon but we only got fifteen.

DAFF (*excited*). We got *fifteen*.

CHRIS. We made cocktails that year.

DAFF (*darkly*). I wouldn't call them that.

CHRIS (*correction*). We... mixed our drinks that year.

They chuckle. They clearly got hammered together.

DAFF. The Jimmy Stewart Cocktail.

CHRIS (*as Jimmy Stewart*). 'Jimmy Stewart'!!

DAFF (*also as Jimmy, pretending to order*). 'Excuse me, bartender!'

CHRIS. 'Excuse me!'

DAFF (*laughing*). Remember Mum? 'Shut up!'

CHRIS. 'Shut up. Go to *bed!*'

DAFF. 'Just go to bed!' I remember when we were kids and we fell out Mum used to make us wear the Make Friends T-shirt –

CHRIS *starts laughing at the memory*.

DAFF (*explains to the audience*). It was one massive T-shirt, and we both had to wear it at the same time and she'd written 'Make Friends' on the front. (*She imitates Mum scrawling angrily on the shirt*.) '*MAKE. FRIENDS*. Just make friends dammit!'

CHRIS. She was like 'I made *two* of you so you would have a friend. You have a friend and you have a friend.'

DAFF. I thought they had me because…

CHRIS. What?

DAFF. I was supposed to fix things.

CHRIS (*mock concern*). No, no. No no no… You were a mistake.

DAFF *playfully tries to wrestle* CHRIS *to the ground. It is surprisingly physical for two grown women*.

Oh my God!

DAFF. Say you're sorry!

CHRIS. Don't mess with me! I'm a mature woman.

CHRIS *drags* DAFF*'s jumper up over her head*. DAFF*'s head disappears from view*. CHRIS *laughs*.

DAFF. Fucking hell!

You're an / asshole.

CHRIS. / Asshole! Jinx.

DAFF *reappears*.

The sisters laugh. They take a breath.

DAFF (*to audience*). Y'know, our mum has a sister, Trudy. They're twins though. And Aunty Trudy was…

How to explain? DAFF *looks to* CHRIS. CHRIS *stares back blankly*.

CHRIS. She was… (*Struggles for something positive*.)

DAFF.…She was our *aunty*.

CHRIS. Yes. Yep.

DAFF. Family.

CHRIS. Yeeeah.

DAFF. Mum said 'I love her, but / she's always –'

CHRIS. / But. 'I love her… *but*'

> (*Complaints they know like the back of their hand*.) 'I love her but she drinks six beers a night.'

DAFF. 'I love her but she never opens the curtains –'

BOTH. '– no wonder she's depressed'.

CHRIS. 'I love her, but she's fucking prickly, don't you think?'

DAFF. Oh shit, she said that?

CHRIS. I said that. I'm saying it to you.

DAFF. I thought they made up!

CHRIS. The last time we left flowers Mum said – she said 'Y'know, she never listened.' And it was… an absolute bummer. It was an absolute, one hundred percent bummer.

DAFF. I wonder if that's why she came up with the Make Friends T-shirt.

CHRIS. She doesn't want me bitching over your grave.

DAFF. I beg your unbelievable pardon?

CHRIS. She's like Bumble. Bumble really held a grudge. Like, you know Bumble hated Uncle Bruce? Uncle Bruce wore glasses. After that Bumble hated everyone with glasses. That's what Mum's like. A proper dog with a bone. The meat is gone but you're hanging on.

DAFF (*nods. To audience*). And that's why you won't meet Dad.

CHRIS (*teasingly to* DAFF). So how's that bone *you're* chewing on?

DAFF (*mock outrage*). Fuck you, man!

The Donation

Several months after the first scene. Mum's house.

The sisters are standing in the doorway to the garden staring out at the night. There is a feeling of staring out at a vast wild scene, trees creaking in the wind. The wind blows through their hair.

CHRIS *has her hands on her abdomen, maybe with a hot-water bottle – she has just had the retrieval procedure that day, she gives off a hectic energy. She breathes in the night.* DAFF *seems unsure of herself.*

CHRIS. I saw Mum walking out here last night.

DAFF. She's spooky isn't / she?

CHRIS. / Such a spooky thing to do. I thought she was a ghost, like… oh my God.

DAFF. She does this as well…

DAFF *demonstrates: opening the collar of her shirt then raising her face to the sky. It is like a movement from a ceremony.*

CHRIS. She does do that!

DAFF. She's a werewolf.

CHRIS. She *is* a werewolf.

CHRIS *considers the garden, she takes deep breaths. Physical discomfort.*

DAFF. You okay?

CHRIS. Yeah, it'll pass. I was just thinking – with a bit of work… I think this garden could be quite beautiful. (*She gestures an area.*) I was reading about this night flowering jasmine that blooms after sunset… (*She looks to the skies, plotting out a design in her mind.*) and if the sun comes in…

Was it Aunty Trudy on the phone?

DAFF *nods with a grimace, this is why Mum was out walking.*

Oh dear.

DAFF. I don't think she approves.

CHRIS. Yeah well… fuck it.

DAFF (*not at all convincingly*). Fuck it.

CHRIS (*with certainty to* DAFF). *Fuck* It.

DAFF. 'I love her *but*…'

CHRIS. I love her but fuck it, they're yours. They're your cavalry.

DAFF. What's the worst thing I've ever done to you?

CHRIS (*slightly taken aback*). Ummm… well you were born.

DAFF (*laughing*). Shut up.

CHRIS. You lost my Sylvanian frog family, I remember that.

DAFF. Oh fuck sake.

CHRIS. The frogs… (*She tuts. Priceless.*)

That's the only time I've been, like, 'Nah. Make Friends T-shirt can't fix this, she's a criminal, just send her to jail.' Beyond that… (*She shrugs.*)

What's the worst thing I've ever done to you?

(*Beat.* DAFF *shakes her head, she cannot think of a single thing.*)

You okay?

DAFF. Yeah.

CHRIS. Yeah?

DAFF *smiles, confidence*.

DAFF. Yes. (*She raises her face to the sky and howls softly like a wolf*.) Hooooowwwwwww!

CHRIS (*joins in*). Hoooowwwwwwww!

DAFF *steals a meaningful look at her sister: she thinks of the eggs*.

DAFF (*shyly*). Thank you.

CHRIS. You're welcome.

SNAP.

Conversation Two

The sisters are side by side addressing the audience again.

DAFF. Ready?

CHRIS *is lost in thought*. DAFF *slaps her playfully/ annoyingly on the face to get her attention*.

CHRIS *looks mock outraged*.

Ready?

CHRIS. Are you?

DAFF (*no. She puts on a brave front*). When I was twenty years old we put fifteen eggs into a company called Genesis. Well, fifteen became fourteen, became thirteen, cause those two were 'poor quality'.

CHRIS. 'Abnormal.'

DAFF. Chris.

CHRIS. Sorry.

DAFF. They *had* said that, from the beginning: that this is the journey, this is what the journey *might* look like, and I was like – 'of course!' Y'know? Of course. But I also remember… I know I had this running catalogue of names just… (*She gestures: a spiraling thought swirling round her ear.*) All their names… (*She cannot keep a straight face, yeek!*)

CHRIS (*seriously*). Yeah but / statistically –

DAFF. / Yeah of course, of *course* like, I know – but… when I let it run… (*Joyful fantasy.*) All these lovely names, just… (*The gorgeous spiral.*) …coming in and out of earshot. Or just before I woke I'd hear a little voice, and I'd be like (*She leans in, speaking tenderly as though to a child.*) 'Wait – say it again… what's your name?'

Alarmingly she reaches out to the unseen dream child.

'Say it again?'

CHRIS. I don't know… (*She feels awkward so resorts to being Robert De Niro.*) 'I don't know, Daphne. Seems unwise.'

DAFF (*joining in as De Niro*). 'It does. It does seem unwise.'

CHRIS. 'It does. To let your mind just… [*run away*], y'know? It really does'. I asked you that Christmas what you were thinking about and you said 'travelling'.

DAFF (*she laughs hopelessly*). I lied.

CHRIS. Yeah but then you left after Christmas.

DAFF (*cheeky grin*). No I didn't, I left after something else.

CHRIS. No you – (*Sudden thought – shit.*) Oh.

DAFF. You've missed something out.

CHRIS (*playing dumb*). Uhhhh… no, no I don't think so?

DAFF. That year / you joined –

CHRIS. / NO. No no. That's all.

DAFF. Go on.

CHRIS (*sigh*). I joined the local theatre.

DAFF points at CHRIS *and laughs.*

(*Defensively.*) It's tough making friends as an adult! Such a turd.

DAFF. I stayed for the play!

CHRIS. She did stay for the play. And what did you say at the end?

DAFF. I said, 'Chris, I loved seeing you on stage.'

CHRIS. Correct. Cause the show was a total plop but I don't need to hear that. Right, so…

DAFF. I go abroad! I take my new body / abroad.

CHRIS (*unimpressed*). / Same body.

DAFF. No, it *looks* the same but, it's like… Old Daff could dance, she was heading in a direction.

(*She points off wildly.*) She had Alan… Alan?

CHRIS (*correction*). *Ian.* You forgot his name!

DAFF. Hey man, that's 'Daphne's' problem.

CHRIS. Who are you then?

DAFF. Out there? (*She points outwards: her mysterious traveling life. With seduction.*)

I was any number of people out there.

CHRIS. Not 'Daphne' then?

DAFF. I just remember walking out of the doctor's office and… (*Shakes head: loss of self.*) I remember Mum said…

Looks to CHRIS, *looking for her to participate.*

Be Mum?

CHRIS. I wasn't there for this.

DAFF. Okay, you be me, and *I'll* be Mum.

CHRIS (*begrudging sigh*). Okay.

They swivel to face each other.

DAFF (*teasing*). Try and look less haggard.

CHRIS. I beg your unbelievable pardon.

DAFF. So Mum said, she said 'Okay if you don't want to be
    Bob Fosse anymore – if that's not you...' She was like
    'Close that page and look somewhere else.' (*Slightly wild*.) I
    remember it like all my roots came away. Like 'Which way
    is the wind blowing? Okay, that's the new North!' Bye Alan –

CHRIS (*correction*). – Ian.

DAFF (*ploughing on*). *Ian* – that's in the past, New Daff is
    going to meet people. New Daff's is like: '*Yes*'. Ask me if I
    meet people? Ask me what New Daff does in her first week
    away.

CHRIS. I'd rather not.

DAFF. She has a threesome.

CHRIS. Daphne.

DAFF. These are –

    *She resorts to the De Niro impression with wagging finger, as
    though this explains everything.*

    'These are the / The Years.'

CHRIS (*reluctantly joining in as De Niro*). / 'That's true. That is
    true'. Is this a Pants Off...?

DAFF. This is a Pants Off story.

CHRIS. Go on then.

DAFF. I remember thinking I had zero reservations.

    Like – what have I got to be shy about, this isn't even my
    body! So I'm standing with this girl, and she's rubbing her
    hand (*Up and down her shoulder.*) like 'Oooh somethings
    going to happen' but when we got back to the room it was
    like (*She gestures, neck upwards.*) Face Only. Like 'ppsst!
    We're straight.' But this *guy* – we bring back this guy called
    Ishmael. He's like (*Smooth.*) 'Call me Ishmael' and we're
    like 'But of course', and then he says – (*Gesturing at 'his'
    crotch.*)

'You know what I call this? You know who this is?'

DAFF *looks to* CHRIS *eagerly for an answer.*

CHRIS (*flatly*). Is it Moby Dick?

DAFF. It is! (*She laughs at the memory.*)

> CHRIS *sighs. She stares out, unimpressed.*

> It was wild! (*She falls flat in retrospect.*) I mean, I *guess* it was wild. Feels a bit like I'm describing something I saw, not something... (*She tails off.*)

CHRIS. Mum worried about you.

DAFF. I know.

CHRIS. 'When is she coming home?'

BOTH. I don't know.

DAFF (*with feeling*). Four years from then... it'll be four years since we were sat in Genesis... I came home on the anniversary of us sitting in that office together.

CHRIS. You're supposed to be looking (*Gestures upwards and about.*) / somewhere else.

DAFF. / Elsewhere, yeah I know.

CHRIS. Just close the page.

DAFF. I am! I am, but the whole time it's like... do you never feel like you're circling something?

> I'm *trying* not to think about them but oh my God, like... (*She gestures, the spiralling thought.*) The fucking *page* y'know?

> So New Daff is out there, she's using a fake name – she's using *Aubrey's* name. And let me tell you, she's dragging that name *right* through the mud –

> S*he clocks* CHRIS, *quietly watching. The joke dies on her lips.*

> *She takes a breath.*

> I take my body to Singapore, New Zealand. Thailand... Canada. (*To* CHRIS.) I missed your thirtieth.

CHRIS. Doesn't matter.

DAFF. How did you spend it?

CHRIS. At home. I was home.

DAFF. Yeah but how did you spend it?

CHRIS. Drinking. I am also home for my thirty-first. And I am home when we lose Bumble.

I used to call him my shadow. He followed me everywhere. He slept on my bed and my God he snored. We had him since we were... (*Gestures self.*) fifteen?

DAFF (*gestures self*). Eight.

CHRIS. And I am home when we lose Aunty Trudy.

Couldn't seem to convince her to stick around, but that's fine.

DAFF. Is it?

CHRIS. To me? Yeah.

DAFF. Did you talk to Mum about it?

CHRIS *nods*.

What did she say?

CHRIS. She said 'When is Daff coming home?'

BOTH. I don't know.

CHRIS. 'Is she looking after herself?'

BOTH (*uneasy and unsure*). I don't know.

CHRIS. 'Is she taking her pills?'

I don't know.

DAFF *is silent*.

Beat. DAFF *considers her sister.*

She had been unaware of CHRIS*'s struggle.*

DAFF (*sings the single high note and waits for* CHRIS *to match it*). Hhhhooooooooooowww!

CHRIS (*instinctively matches the note*). Hoooooooowwww.

What was that?

DAFF. Just checking. Were you lonely?

CHRIS shakes her head.

Talk about yourself.

CHRIS scoffs – no.

To her alarm DAFF *walks offstage and sits in the front row facing* CHRIS.

CHRIS. Oh my God what the hell!?

DAFF. Say three things about yourself.

CHRIS (*hesitating*). Uhhhhh.

DAFF. Do it!

CHRIS. Okay (*Awkward. Struggles to think of things: One.*)…

So… yeah, alright – so I look after – I've been looking after the garden and the first – I'm planting – and the first thing I planted was Pennyroyal. Which is – it's this medicinal, sort of mint – but it's also, it can be poisonous – if you take it in the wrong – like… it can be – it's lethal, in a – you make tea, and then… umm. (*Two.*) If you burn yourself, and you take a sprig of lavender, like the flowers – and if you tape that over the burn then it / won't blister. Ummm… (*Three.*)

DAFF (*cutting in from the audience*). / Booooooo!

CHRIS. Oh my God, what?

DAFF. I said talk about yourself.

CHRIS. I am!

DAFF comes back to her seat onstage, muttering.

DAFF. You're shit at that.

CHRIS. That was interesting stuff!

DAFF. Why are you growing poison in the garden?

CHRIS. It's not poison, it's a mint. I don't want to do this anymore.

DAFF. What was the third thing? Any third thing about yourself.

CHRIS. The week we lost Bumble I got diagnosed with Arrhythmia.

And Mum said 'I'm sorry' and I said 'Why are you sorry?' and she said 'Cause I've got that.' I was standing in the workshop, and then Drew took me to A and E.

DAFF. Disorganised / heartbeat.

CHRIS. / Disorganised heartbeat. Seems so stupid, over a dog.

Drew

DAFF. And just like that we meet Drew.

DAFF *and* CHRIS *smile at each other with understanding – uncomfortable territory ahead. They attempt to remain impartial and playful.*

Describe the person you know.

CHRIS. Describe the / person *you* know.

DAFF. / No, describe the person *you* know.

CHRIS. Okay... Drew was working at Hubbards when I started working there.

We took over the business together. We rebranded / it as the Night...

DAFF. / No, describe *him* though. Like, the physical human being.

CHRIS. He drives a pick-up.

DAFF. I mean describe him like you would describe a person to the police: Like 'six-five, dark hair...'

CHRIS. Okay... (*Blank.*)

DAFF. You're *dreadful* at this! He was your best friend, right?

CHRIS. Yeah.

DAFF. *Describe* him. Is he easy to talk to? What kind of flower would he be? Does he have a hook for a hand?

CHRIS *looks sceptical.*

They're not going to meet him so... You should be able to *describe* a person. If you *really* know / someone –

CHRIS. / Alright, yeah, yeah okay: Yes. I think... yeah, he *is* easy to talk to. I think, probably he'd be... he'd be a dandelion. He has *two* hands.

He's a big person but he stoops. He's awkward, until you get to know him. He mainly listens which I think might come across as a bit standoffish. He stands in the doorway unless you invite him into the room. When he eats an apple he eats it from the bottom up and he eats the whole thing, the stalk – and he has a silent laugh... like a (*She demonstrates a breathy, Muttley-style 'hehehe'.*) Would you say this is accurate?

DAFF (*unreadable*)....Yup.

CHRIS. I think if you were stranded in town Drew is the kind of guy who'd come and get you.

DAFF. Like a rescue?

CHRIS. Yeah. If you were drunk in town, like... if you were hanging off a statue of Lady Godiva, in need of a friend, I think Drew would come and get you.

DAFF. You think it or you know it?

CHRIS. I know it.

And then he'd sleep on the sofa, and *then* he'd have breakfast with Mum, then he'd take you to McDonalds. And then he'd eat your McMuffin.

DAFF. Is he handsome?

CHRIS....He's a contract gardener.

DAFF. That's not an answer! Is he hot?

CHRIS. No. / Well –

DAFF. / Is he ugly?

CHRIS. No! I'd say… he *is* attractive because of his 'way'.

He's got a very attractive 'way' about him – that's what I think.

DAFF *looks highly doubtful*.

He thinks he's ugly.

DAFF. Is he?

CHRIS. No!

DAFF. Have you ever tried it on?

CHRIS. He's my friend.

DAFF (*barbed*). Does he know that?

Beat.

CHRIS. D'you know Aubrey asked me that.

She came round when you were traveling. I found her in my workshop talking to Drew.

DAFF. What did you do?

CHRIS. I shooed her away. I was like (*Big energy.*) 'Get out of here, go on GET OUT OF HERE!'

The sisters laugh at the thought.

DAFF. What did you really do?

CHRIS. I waited, didn't I. And then she just… wafted off.

DAFF. I didn't know she came round.

CHRIS. Got to throw her knives at someone hasn't she.

DAFF. She say something mean?

CHRIS. Yeah, she called me a 'homebird' and then when I laughed at something she said 'You've got crows feet.'

DAFF. I'm sorry.

CHRIS (*darkly*). I could describe *her* if you like?

DAFF. What did she want?

CHRIS. She wanted to know when Daff was coming home.

DAFF. But / I don't know.

CHRIS. / 'I don't know.'

How to reconnect to each other? DAFF *steps up.*

DAFF. Do you remember what I did the day I got home?

CHRIS. Yeah, you told me you'd lost my camera.

DAFF. No, I did this –

DAFF *immediately steps over with her jumper raised to hoop it over* CHRIS*'s head, like* CHRIS *had done for her in the first scene.*

CHRIS. No, that's –

Too late, she is now in the jumper with DAFF.

SNAP.

Daff's Return

As before, DAFF *has* CHRIS *enveloped in her jumper. They hold each other tightly.*

DAFF. I lost your camera.

CHRIS (*from within the jumper*). I traded in your car and I kept the money.

DAFF. I gave your name at a key party.

CHRIS. I missed you.

DAFF *holds* CHRIS *tighter.*

DAFF. I missed you too.

SNAP.

Conversation Three

Addressing the audience with purpose:

DAFF (*cheeky*). Okay so here's how *I'd* describe Drew.

(*Pointedly*.) I'm about to tell a pants off story.

CHRIS *trudges off stage muttering under her breath*.

CHRIS. Fucking hell.

DAFF. So Chris was working at Hubbards.

DAFF *sits alone*.

CHRIS (*shouting in from offstage*). It wasn't called Hubbards by then.

DAFF. Go on.

CHRIS (*reappearing round the door*). It's called The Night Garden.

DAFF. And you've got a workshop in the garage?

CHRIS. Yeah but you're not allowed in there.

DAFF *turns back to the audience looking extremely cheeky*.

DAFF. Yes I am. He's not ugly y'know.

CHRIS. I never – !

Why bother? She exits leaving DAFF on stage alone.

Daff Alone

She looks out at the audience mischievously.

DAFF. Chris and Drew did all this work on Mum's garden while I was away.

Like, you can tell it's going to look nice. And Drew does a lot of woodwork out of the garage. He follows Chris round like a massive shadow. And I mean, he's a *beast* but he always brings these little packed lunches, and he'll offer you coffee from his thermos even though the kitchen is, like – it's just inside. And he'll give you the nice cup. The *nice* cup. And he'll look at you like... you can feel him looking at you. And you can feel him wondering what on *earth* to do about it. He'll be peeping over the brim. He'll be looking at you like... (*To be wanted, exhilarating.*) I don't know how to describe it.

He's got a really nice *way* about him. He's a gentleman. In a monster body.

He makes this thing at the nursery called a fairy garden. It's like a tiny garden in a jar, and if kids bring in their own jar he shows them how to make it. He helps them pick out the moss and what kind of flowers...

Breathtakingly cute. She shakes her head and laughs.

So stupid.

Beat. She is frustrated with herself.

I didn't want... I didn't think I was looking, but... he'd make a good dad, y'know? (*She hangs her head, quietly.*) Fuck.

Y'know, I have this friend who bragged that she has never changed. Her body... is the same. She still wears the clothes of her youth, because she has the body of a teenager. And I thought (*Repulsed.*) 'Eugh!' Like (*Thumbs up.*) 'Great, well done!' but *eugh*, fuck you. I won't tell you the person's name because it's not the brag that bothers me, it's just... what are you supposed to say to that?

Because I *have* changed. I don't recognise this [*body*] so much anymore. I mean, it's *familiar,* but we don't *communicate*. (*She laughs.*) It's just static, that's the only sound... static.

She amuses herself in her struggle to explain. Shame bubbles beneath.

I think of my body like... it's stubborn. Like... we're not
good friends. I think of my body sometimes like it's a spooky
hotel, and I'm just haunting it. I was a guest in the hotel, and
then I died. (*She chuckles – grim.*)

Cause no one lives in a hotel, you just pass through it. You go
there to fuck around and then... you go home.

Beat.

My doctor *was* right, he said... (*Hard to say.*) He said your
libido might go. He said it's mainly a psychological thing,
cause if you don't feel your best then you don't always
want... like, you don't *want*, necessarily. But I thought 'No,
(*Forcefully arguing with her body.*) I'm the boss. The brain
is the boss so you'll (*Gestures roughly to body.*) do what I
tell you to do. I'm going to *tell* you that you want this.' You
know? (*She tries to joke.*) 'I run this hotel!'

I never tell the friend any of this. I let her brag and show
me photos of her kid like – 'Look at my kid. Look at them
naked. Look at *ME* naked', like... 'Look at us. (*Lavish.*) Just
look.'

But I keep the friend because... I want to say loyalty? But I
think the answer is self-harm. Cause I let her.

Beat. A guilty confession.

Her daughter *is* beautiful.

In my darkest moments I wish upon her unexceptional kids.
Snotty little, fucking reprobate kids. Like, bottom of the
class, no friends...

*Try as she might it's impossible to make these things sound
negative.*

But I don't. I don't. I wish that for *me*.

I wish... I wish I could be with Drew like I was with others.
I wish it didn't mean anything, I think. Just fuck around and
then go home. But, he's a... (*please understand*) a 'dad',
y'know?

So we sit in Genesis and we say… (*She nods: anxious, the first egg.*) 'Okay.' We're like 'Yeah, we're going to do this.' Like… 'In we go!'

She chuckles darkly.

They talk about 'quality'. Like… the quality of the eggs and they talk about what would make it *viable*. And I was like: 'Well that's great: Thirteen. That's a head start.' But only ten of them will fertilise and from that ten only six will have Grade One viability. You'd wait for that morning call from the clinic, like: 'Eight is gone. Seven is gone. Six…'

She hold her hands as though steadying a table, awaiting more loss, but the eggs hold.

And I think, okay… six.

She rallies up some defiance.

That's still a head start.

And I wish on them. I wish on that first one.

I dream about them. But in my dreams I am a whale, and I'm pregnant with a cub. In the moment before birth I say 'When you are born I will teach you to dive. I'll teach you to leap out of the waves and to sing.'

But I give birth to a wolf.

If I dive beneath the water the wolf will drown, but if I rise above the surface I will suffocate. So I glide along with the wolf on my back. And the wolf grows hungry. I try to feed it the food I eat, I feed it plankton and shrimp and stuff, but the wolf grows hungry. I give it the food out of my mouth, but the wolf grows hungry. It stands on my back and it howls, and the howl echoes down my blowhole. So I cut out my tongue and the wolf eats that. And I cut out my heart and the wolf eats that. As my body drifts onto the shore the wolf steps onto the land, and then it runs into the woods.

Beat. CHRIS *reappears.*

CHRIS. You talking about Aubrey?

DAFF. I was trying / not to.

CHRIS (*out to audience*). / She is a biiiiiitttttch.

DAFF. Chris.

CHRIS. Did you tell them she sent a photo of herself in labor?

Mid labor. Like a pig in the butcher.

Then she came round here and she said all this shit about weight loss? Like, here's us: all mince pies, and she's like (*Scathing impression of Aubrey.*) 'I've never been more thin! Pregnancy weight – where's it gone?!' And I was like: that's exactly what happens in *Rosemary's Baby*, and you know what she gave birth to…? Satan.

DAFF (*quiet. It's too much*). Chris –

CHRIS. – No, and then right, listen: She introduced the baby: this is baby Clementina. 'Clementina'… just let that sink in. But then she said, she said 'You know what… I hate the nickname Tina. It's ever so trashy. *Tina*. So trashy.'

DAFF. Chris –

CHRIS (*she ploughs on with increasing rage*). She's just – I think she's tactless. I think she's / she's –

DAFF. / Chris.

CHRIS. / – her insecurity is – I think it makes her cruel? I think – I don't think she's / oblivious –

DAFF. / Chris /

CHRIS. / I think she's /

DAFF. / Chris /

CHRIS. / I think she's a fucking asshole. That's what I think. I think she's an inconsiderate fucking – self-centred…

CHRIS *looks to* DAFF. DAFF *sits desolate*.

CHRIS *reaches out for* DAFF.

The sisters hold hands across the space.

What are you thinking?

DAFF *gestures, the spiraling thought: baby names.*

I told you not to name them.

DAFF. You did, you did say that. Y'know Aubrey wouldn't have known, I was only three weeks in.

No one would've known… (*Softly.*) Robin.

CHRIS *shakes her head.*

The Babies

DAFF. Why did you tell me not to name them?

CHRIS. I thought it would make life harder.

DAFF.…You planted something for me.

CHRIS. No, I just planted some*thing*. A cherry tree.

DAFF. It's always full of robins.

CHRIS *shrugs it off.*

Then there was Glenn the following year. Glenn didn't survive storage. And then Gale… Gale made it out of the freezer, but wouldn't take. I think that's when we stopped talking about it. Me and Drew. We didn't *stop,* we just stopped *talking* about it.

Gale wasn't even a blip.

DAFF *looks to* CHRIS *for detail.*

What did you plant?

CHRIS (*almost shamefully*). Glen Ample Raspberry and a Willow.

DAFF. What's the Willow called?

CHRIS. Myrica Gale Sweet Willow, is the… [*full name*]

DAFF (*quietly*). Gale.

> DAFF *shakes her head with a sigh: 'I'll process that later.'*

> Drew always made me feel like... I filled up the room. The way I moved.

> I felt graceful in comparison I guess. I asked him what he wanted and he said 'I want you to have what *you* want'. Which is not quite the same as saying 'I want the same thing', is it?

> Like, I want this *with* you. I know by that point I could count them on one hand...

> *An open palm. She curls her hand into a fist.*

> I remember hitting him.

> He must have told you that?

CHRIS. He didn't talk about it.

DAFF. It took five years to make Ashley. She stayed just long enough that you could hear her heartbeat. She sounded like... (*Bittersweet.*) cosmic space noise. Like... (*Hard to describe, she tries to replicate, throbbing sonar.*)

> Like a satellite passing by. (*Throbbing sonar growing fainter as it sails overhead.*) And then... I shoved him. Like, I really shoved him. He fell into a cabinet and it cracked the glass. He said it didn't hurt... not in that way. He'd say 'I love you' and I thought: That doesn't help me. Say something else.

> Ashley... my winter baby.

> *DAFF looks to* CHRIS. *An unspoken question.*

CHRIS. Snowdrops.

DAFF. That was the year I lost Drew.

> CHRIS *awkwardly makes to go*.

CHRIS. You want me out for this?

DAFF (*matter of factly*). No. No no no... No.

CHRIS *remains, listening quietly.*

She presses her heart discreetly, stress induced arrhythmia.

DAFF *sees* CHRIS *pressing on her heart.*

Arrhythmia?

CHRIS. It's fine.

DAFF. You gave him money from The Night Garden I know, for Gale.

For others as well, was that you?

CHRIS *nods gently – yes.*

And yet he didn't talk about it? I find that hard to believe.

CHRIS (*unwilling*). We didn't talk about it.

DAFF. But you did *talk* though. Did he tell you we tried again?

CHRIS *looks away – yes.*

Well fucking hell. What did he tell you?

CHRIS. Just the name... Riley.

DAFF. Y'know I always thought you would have made a good pair, you and Drew.

And I was right.

For a moment CHRIS *sits tensely, she then abruptly gets up.*

She kisses DAFF *on the forehead and starts back to her seat in the audience.*

DAFF *watches her coldly.*

Where are you going?

CHRIS. It's your story.

DAFF. I asked you to stay. I want to know what you think.

CHRIS. I think you should have talked to Mum.

DAFF. I did. But I want to know what *you* think.

CHRIS (*beat*). I thought –

DAFF. Oh, you *do* have a thought?

CHRIS (*treading carefully*). I thought… I felt that – for you…

DAFF (*harshly*). Get your words out.

CHRIS. I wanted you to stop. What did Mum say?

DAFF. She said she'd always loved the name Jude.

    CHRIS *shakes her head with disapproval: enabler.*

    She finds a seat near the front.

So, what? Am I telling this without you?

CHRIS. I'm still here. I'm throwing distance.

    DAFF *suddenly slips off her shoe and throws it bitterly at*
    CHRIS *in the audience.* CHRIS *looks calmly from the shoe*
    back to her sister.

See?

    DAFF *stares at* CHRIS, *stone faced, she then speaks to the*
    audience whilst maintaining frosty eye contact with CHRIS.

DAFF. When I think of Chris this is how I picture her: sitting on
the sidelines.

    Look round to audience.

Oh, I'm sorry – I should say, she is a part of this. She's quite
a big part.

CHRIS. I'm still here, Daphne.

DAFF. Are you?

    Time to burn some bridges.

Chris never brings any boyfriends home and me and Mum
never ask about it and you'd think that was a conversation in
itself, that we understand something about her. And the fact
we're not saying anything means we're waiting for *her* to say
something.

    CHRIS *sinks into her seat, horrified.*

I'm sorry, but you learn all this stuff about me and you learn hardly one thing about her. (*To* CHRIS.) You *and* Drew, you're like a pair of fucking Easter Island heads!

CHRIS. What d'you want me to say?

DAFF. Tell me to stop! If you think I should stop then say that. Say stop!!

CHRIS. It's not my place.

DAFF. *Then whose is it?!*

Beat.

(*With disdain.*) You know you paint this picture of yourself as this groveling pauper who lives on my estate. Some sort of fucking fish head pauper, but you are a part of this and you *could* sit here (*Indicates on stage.*) if you wanted to.

CHRIS. I *don't* want to. I don't like being up there.

DAFF. What did you like about him in that moment?

CHRIS (*not playing*). Daphne –

DAFF. What did you *like* about him? Must have been something.

You went back in the closet for him.

CHRIS. I'm / not *in* the –

DAFF. / Were you trying to prove something about yourself?

CHRIS. It didn't mean anything. (*She's lying.*)

DAFF. Does *he* know that?

CHRIS. You know what, what do *you* like about him, Daphne? Tell me how it feels to hit someone that you like. (*Beat.*) Y'know I wish I had said something. I *wish* I'd had the nuts to say something, I mean I love you Daff but...

DAFF. But?

CHRIS. I just, I didn't know, like – who am I supposed to defend?

DAFF. What a cowardly thing to say.

CHRIS. You're never satisfied –

DAFF. You're so fucking yellow.

CHRIS (*she snaps*). And you're selfish. What a selfish person.

(*Beat, she went too far.*) I love you Daphne.

DAFF. 'But.'

CHRIS. I love you.

DAFF. I love you 'but'.

DAFF *stands abruptly.*

Stand there. (*Indicates beside her on the stage.*)

CHRIS. I don't want to.

DAFF (*presentation*). That year Chris stood there.

DAFF *points opposite herself.* CHRIS *reluctantly rejoins on stage.*

She hands her thrown shoe back to DAFF *but doesn't let go – a brief tug of war. There is an atmosphere of threat. They reenact The Slap.*

DAFF. Ready?

CHRIS. No.

DAFF. Three. Two. One –

Suddenly DAFF *slaps* CHRIS *lightly on the cheek.* CHRIS *openly laughs with disbelief at this poor imitation of a slap she once received. As* DAFF *goes to retract her hand,* CHRIS *catches her wrist firmly and holds it tight. She speaks fiercely as she repeats The Slap.*

CHRIS. Three, two, one.

CHRIS *brings* DAFF's *hand back up to her face with significant force. SLAP!*

Unbidden, DAFF *gasps.*

DAFF. I never hit you that hard.

CHRIS (*stating it plainly*). It was harder. You were violent. You were a violent person.

The Slap

We are back at The Slap as it happened.

The sisters stand as before. A stormy atmosphere.

CHRIS. Did Drew tell you why he left?

DAFF. No, he didn't.

CHRIS. Would you like *me* to tell you?

> DAFF *considers* CHRIS *for a second looking unnervingly calm.*

> *She then lashes out fiercely, backhanding* CHRIS *hard across the face.*

> *SMACK!*

> *SNAP out of conversation mode.* DAFF *sees her violence as though through clear eyes. She is horrified. She goes to* CHRIS*'s side.*

DAFF. I'm so sorry, Chris.

> CHRIS *holds* DAFF *at bay and says, flatly.*

CHRIS. That's it. That was you.

> *The sisters tentatively try to console each other. They attempt an embrace, to forgive the horrible years. It doesn't succeed.* CHRIS *fails to keep a mortified* DAFF *onstage.*

DAFF. It's all yours.

> DAFF *slinks offstage.*

Chris Alone

CHRIS *stands alone.*

Any Christmas lights still on stage flicker out.

She toys shamefully with some of the decorations and tries hard not to cry.

She quietly sings the final chorus from Gloria Estefan's 'Anything for You' to give herself time to think. She avoids eye contact with the audience. Her singing is wobbly. She prays for DAFF*'s return but the song fizzles out and she is still alone on stage.*

The moon rises on a night garden. We see a fraction of the whole, a garden that must be really beautiful seen in full. A moon above.

CHRIS. I know that, I'm – I remember when I left... I hang up on Daff and she hangs up on me. Drew left. He did leave. They had one egg left, I know, but we didn't talk about it. He sold me back his shares and... that was, I think that was a very kind thing to do.

I move out. I moved out.

Somewhere in that house is the Make Friends T-shirt...

She shrugs.

She takes a breath and looks around.

I miss this garden. The workshop.

Beat. She looks about the garden with hope.

I planted Lady of the Night, Evening Primrose, Lupin, Brugmansia, Moonflower... Riley Maple. And then I miss four years of watching them all bloom. Four years is a really long time. I bet it really came alive out here.

She takes a breath.

The next time I saw Daphne she was in the hospital, she was sitting outside Mum's room with a cup of coffee and it... I mean, she was sitting like – she just looked... (*Heartbroken*.) It was a super shit day. Super shit.

Daff got married! She had met someone and... she got married, in the –

She shakes her head and tuts: so much time lost.

We were sitting in shifts. Outside of... for Mum, outside Mum's room. And we had a lot of, oh God – such horrible coffee. It was like, really weak but it was also really gritty, like, it all sank and it didn't mix. It was just slush.

It was a... she had a heart attack.

Feeling strangled, she pulls her collar open.

Mum always said she couldn't think straight inside. Like, inside a building. And we joked that her thoughts were vertical and that the roof was in the way. Cause her thoughts go up.

She takes a breath and raises her face to the sky. Werewolf.

She speaks to Mum.

You liked that I was a gardener so I – I mean, I *love* doing the gardens. I love it.

You liked walking in the dark, so I thought – the nursery is... it's called The Night Garden. You liked children, so I host a weekend workshop for kids. I teach them about seeds and bugs and stuff and I never told you that I'm queer and I never introduced you to Carolyn. She started working in The Night Garden and I never told you who she was. You said 'Please don't be lonely' and I never told you 'Well, (*Nodding to Carolyn*.) y'know, Carolyn comes home with me, so...' You asked me who I spent Christmas with. I spent it with Carolyn. We made a proper Christmas dinner and she told me to invite you. She said 'ask your mum. Ask your sister. Just ask them to come,' and I... I didn't know what to do. I'm so fucking yellow.

She shakes her head, her regrets are palpable. She takes a breath.

My best seller is the Camellia and my flop is the Purple Aeonium. I think they're beautiful but Carolyn says it looks like an evil daisy. I sell roses. People always want them so we sell – we have quite a range. I sell a rose called Jude, which has peach... the Jude rose is peach. I sell that.

If I could go back, if I could give myself some advice...

She hesitates, then shakes her head: too painful to imagine.

I regret how it looked that day for Daff. It looked like we had something that she didn't, and I guess we did. Cause I did kiss him. And it did mean something. I was trying to tell him he was worthwhile.

He cast a very warm shadow. And I would've been happy living in it, I think. Like... I would've been happy enough. But I work with plants, and plants lean into the sun. Before Carolyn... I would be standing outside and when the sun came out, I'd see my shadow and I'd be like: well, that's proof then. There I am.

I speak with Daff sometimes on the phone – well... we 'check in'. And she says 'Do you need anything, Christine?' and... I mean, that's proof. That I'm there. But we don't talk. I wish – it would... sorry, Daff's better at – (*She gestures: speaking. She laughs, ironic.*) She's better at this.

I think... I think I just went missing. I think that's probably what happened but I don't know. You'd have to ask her.

The Night Garden

The present. Christmas Eve. Moonlight.

CHRIS *stands central in the garden wearing an anorak.*

DAFF *appears wearing a blanket, she carries a bottle of wine.*

CHRIS *begins to sing the high pitched opening harmonies to The Beach Boys' 'Don't Worry Baby' – a song they both know by heart.*

DAFF *stares, sceptical, as* CHRIS *struggles with note –*

DAFF. Why are you singing it that high?

CHRIS. This is the pitch – (*She continues the harmony, waiting for* DAFF *to join in with the supporting tune. She speaks in a singing voice.*) Are-you-going-to-join-in-or-what?

DAFF *reluctantly joins in, harmonising. They sing their mother's favourite song until they reach the end of the chorus.*

They fall into awkward silence.

DAFF *pours them a drink. All is not well.*

Why did you sing it so high?

CHRIS. That's the pitch.

DAFF. Mum never sang it that high.

CHRIS. Yeah, but The Beach Boys did.

Beat. DAFF *sings the following chorus quietly at a lower, easier pitch.*

CHRIS *joins in.*

They stare up at the house.

Aubrey's getting divorced.

CHRIS (*interest piqued*). Is she?!

DAFF. A friend told me. He had an affair.

CHRIS. What do you think?

DAFF. I think a good friend would have sympathy.

CHRIS. Right. So what do *you* think?

DAFF *smiles grimly.*

DAFF. Touché. She did reach out but... I don't know. She said
Dylan was 'awkward'. She said 'Oh, it's hard enough being
a mother but being a *step*-mother! I mean (*In awe.*) Bravo
Daphne, bravo.' And then she called him awkward. She said
he was an 'awkward little boy'. She said all this stuff about
'baby on the chest'. Like (*A fawning Aubrey impression.*)
'I still feel Clementina... (*Heart.*) right here, y'know? And
when the mother *hasn't* – like, that neglect... you can always
tell.'

All those years of friendship – dead. (*Snaps fingers.*) Just like
that. Cause Dylan...

She looks to the house, Dylan's bedroom.

Dylan is my boy.

CHRIS. Have you run out of energy to be mad at her?

DAFF. Guess so.

CHRIS. Run out of energy to be mad at me?

*DAFF looks to CHRIS, no answer. They stare back up at the
house.*

CHRIS speaks with revulsion.

Clementina.

DAFF. Tina.

CHRIS. 'So trashy'.

House looks nice.

DAFF grins despite herself. Beat.

DAFF. We moved into Mum's room – *our* room, and... (*She
points up at a window.*) your room –

CHRIS. Dylan's room. Does he like the clouds on the ceiling?

Beat. Clearly DAFF has removed them.

Did you keep *anything* of mine?

DAFF. I did.

Beat.

CHRIS. He's a nice little boy.

DAFF. He is.

CHRIS. I don't think he's awkward.

DAFF (*with motherly passion*). He's not! Connor is an awesome dad. I think he did a great job.

CHRIS. And you said it would never last.

DAFF (*oops*). I *did* say that. I was really gunning for a one night stand but Connor just… ruined it. I was like 'Chop chop take your pants off, let's be having it' and he was like 'Tell me about yourself. Can I make you dinner? Do you like the zoo? Here's my son!' He bought me a glow in the dark solar system for my birthday… (*She shakes her head lovingly.*) What a sap.

Connor is like… the string on a kite? And up there… (*Gestures: flying in the air.*)

CHRIS. Dylan?

DAFF *nods. Full of love.*

What does he call you?

DAFF. 'My Daphne.'

CHRIS. My Daphne.

DAFF (*a beloved exchange*). 'I'm saving a slice for my Daphne.'

They smile to each other. Understanding.

How's Carol?

CHRIS. Carolyn.

DAFF (*fuck*). How's Carolyn?

You could have brought her.

CHRIS. You know, it…

CHRIS *looks to* DAFF.

CHRIS *stares at the house.*

She trails off. DAFF *waits patiently, with kindness.*

DAFF. Say something about yourself.

CHRIS. I was telling Carolyn…

She shakes her head. A stupid memory.

I used to – I don't know if they did this in your year but we used to swap stickers in school. And I was telling Carolyn how I'd drawn this… I drew this naked lady in the back of my – in the sticker album, like, on the – inside the cover. And I was sent to the teacher. And I remember standing in the classroom and he was holding the album, and there's the lady – (*Embarrassed.*) Hello! And then he just – he turned the page and he said (*Confidentially.*) 'Let's just put a paperclip over this.'

DAFF. How old were you?

CHRIS. Eight? Mr Flude.

DAFF. What was the drawing like?

CHRIS. The lady? She was stood like this –

A stiff walking pose.

With this –

She points her fingers: two straight-shooting nipples. Her laugh fades.

DAFF. You could have told Mum about Carolyn, she wouldn't have judged you.

CHRIS. I know.

DAFF. You're the one / who didn't give her the chance.

CHRIS (*riled and unwilling to hear it*). / I know. I know!

DAFF *offers the bottle,* CHRIS *reluctantly holds her glass out for a refill.*

DAFF. I really like Carolyn. She's a very cool cucumber.

CHRIS (*smiling*). She is.

DAFF. Does she help you with the nursery?

CHRIS. She does. She laughs at me cause I talk to the plants, but ever so often I catch *her* doing it, and I'm like (*An ambush.*) 'What are you telling them!? Are you talking about me!'

The sisters chuckle together.

I asked her to marry me last year.

DAFF*'s face drops.*

I should have said but... *you* didn't say.

DAFF. I did tell you.

CHRIS. No, I found out from Mum.

DAFF. We should try and do better, really.

CHRIS. Yeah, we should... Mum hated this.

DAFF. We'll do better. We will, we'll do better. I mean... Dylan doesn't have an aunty. *Aunties*. But, a bit more family, maybe...

CHRIS. Yeah?

DAFF. Yeah. I know he rebelled a bit at the start. Y'know, new home, new... person. And I – I still have baths for my fatigue and... he went through a phase of flinging stuff into the bath before I could get in it. Like bread, or the bog brush. And I was like... (*She nods, thoroughly amused.*) 'Well played, young man.'

But now, he... (*She smiles, heart full.*)

CHRIS. 'My Daphne.'

DAFF. Yeah... What do you hope?

CHRIS. Y'know, I've reached an age where I just really hope I'm not going to grow a beard, but...

(*Strokes her chin suspiciously.*) We'll see.

DAFF *laughs, they are starting to soften.*

DAFF. I'm hoping I don't have to join the PTA. I can feel they're going to ask me, and I *know* I'm just going to fold.

CHRIS. I hope my knees stop crunching. Every time I stand up it's like someone snapping a Kit Kat.

DAFF. I hope we get better on the phone.

CHRIS. Yeah.

DAFF. You know where you are with a grudge.

CHRIS. Yeah.

DAFF. It's like a tire fire. It just burns.

CHRIS. I'm hoping...

CHRIS *swallows her words and looks away awkwardly.*
DAFF *eyes her curiously.*

You know, Carolyn runs the workshops, the nature workshops, if Dylan... I don't know if that's his cup of tea?

DAFF. Yeah?

CHRIS. She's really good with children.

DAFF *nods kindly, non-committal.*

We had talked a few times about... y'know, your friends get married and – so you have conversations like: 'Is that something? Would you ever?' Like... here's a conversation full of booby traps. Like, *someone* is going to trip up and say how they really feel. And so I was saying like: Oh, y'know I don't think I think ahead? I think I have trouble picturing myself anywhere in advance', and Carolyn said... she said 'Well just so you know, I *do* think ahead, and I think of you.' And it was like... the needle just stopped spinning.

I thought: the sun is going to come up and I'm going to ask her to marry me.

And the next day we're at The Night Garden. It's like... grey dawn, and we're setting up and I see Carolyn and she looked over at me and she's like (*Suspicious.*) 'What are you looking at?' so I... (*She laughs.*) yeah, I mean... that's how I asked her. I proposed, without a ring, at work, and she told me later that she was standing by the compost, but the sun was coming up...

All day I saw her and I thought, I can't believe… I can't believe I'm here.

CHRIS, *filled with weird energy, chugs her glass of wine then begins something that feels pre-prepared.*

Carolyn is forty-nine. When she was single she used to take herself out for dinner. If you're thinking on your feet Carolyn always walks with you. If someone interrupts you in a group she always asks 'What is it you were you saying / before someone interrupted –'

DAFF (*cutting in*). / What are you doing?

CHRIS. I'm describing / Carolyn.

DAFF. / Yeah I know, I've met her.

CHRIS. I saw from Mum's estate that she's still paying the bills for Genesis, and I wanted – I'm just, I wondered… (*Deep breath.*) who's left?

DAFF *looks stricken.*

DAFF. Oh my God.

CHRIS. I'm sorry.

DAFF (*whispering*). Oh my God.

CHRIS. I thought I knew myself better than this, I'm sorry.

DAFF. Look elsewhere, I swear to God –

CHRIS. I don't want to look elsewhere.

A challenging silence.

DAFF. I can't believe… y'know I asked Mum about this. I was like 'What if' You know? What if you turn up… and you ask for them? What am I… what will I do?!

Cause it'll work for you. It'll be like, this whole time they just wanted to come home.

CHRIS. I just wanted to know who.

DAFF. You told me not to name them.

CHRIS. Yeah, but you did it anyway.

Tension. They stare daggers.

DAFF. I threw out your stuff when you left. I threw it all out. I was relentless about it.

CHRIS. I know.

DAFF. I scraped us out of the house.

CHRIS. I deleted you off my phone.

DAFF. I threw out the Make Friends T-shirt.

CHRIS (*genuinely stunned*). Oh, well we're screwed then.

DAFF *watches* CHRIS *coldly wanting to judge her reaction as she levels* CHRIS *with an awful test. What follows is a lie and* DAFF *knows it.*

DAFF. I tried again without you.

Without Drew.

But they didn't make it out of the dish. They said 'It's faltered.' They said 'Sorry, sometimes this is just the journey.'

CHRIS *swallows hard and sinks into a seat, the dream is dashed.*

Are you thinking what you'll tell Carolyn?

CHRIS *nods – yes.*

I *wanted* to stop after Drew, but… I'm selfish.

Do you regret coming now?

CHRIS (*shaking her head sadly*). No.

DAFF (*stiffly*). No?

CHRIS.…

Softly. She takes in her sister.

No.

Beat.

DAFF. You know Mum used to walk in this garden, and I do that. You spent a lot of time out here.

CHRIS. I did.

DAFF. Are you going to watch *It's a Wonderful Life* this year?

CHRIS (*nods helplessly. A line from the film, Jimmy. Quietly*). 'I want to live!'

DAFF (*unreadable*). It was a flop when it first came out.

CHRIS. I know. It's unbelievable.

　　DAFF *takes a deep breath. It is time to let* CHRIS *in.*

DAFF. You should ask me again who's left. You said I hope. 'I'm hoping'...

　　Beat. CHRIS *tenses, hardly daring.*

　　...Jude. Jude is left.

CHRIS (*release. She samples the name like nectar*). 'Jude.' That's lovely.

　　The sisters finally see each other.

　　I miss Mum.

DAFF. I miss you.

　　I missed my friend.

CHRIS (*smiles, bittersweet*). 'I made you a friend –'

BOTH. '– and I made *you* a friend.'

　　The sisters smile at each other: love.

DAFF. I love this garden.

CHRIS. Me too.

　　DAFF *gazes up at the window: Dylan. She seems at peace.*

DAFF. I am lucky.

CHRIS. You are lucky.

CHRIS *raises her head to the night, she is the first to howl.*

DAFF *immediately matches her.*

They howl softly into the night. A long and haunting sound.

The release of years of tension. It is almost a sound of grief.

BOTH. *Hoooooooooooooooooowwwwwwwwwww!*

CHRIS. What will the neighbours think?!

DAFF (*laughs*). Fuck it.

Ready?

(*Toasts.*) This year.

BOTH. This year.

CHRIS (*hope*). Jude.

Under the moonlight the garden comes alive in full, we see it expand in shades of blue and white. We see the night above, the stars. We hear the soft chorus of night birds, the sound of the wind through the leaves. The full beauty of the garden enveloping the space.

A wild and beautiful Eden.

Lights down.

A Nick Hern Book

Pennyroyal first published in Great Britain as a paperback original in 2022 by Nick Hern Books Limited, The Glasshouse, 49a Goldhawk Road, London W12 8QP, in association with Jessie Anand Productions and the Finborough Theatre, London

Pennyroyal copyright © 2022 Lucy Roslyn

Lucy Roslyn has asserted her right to be identified as the author of this work

Cover image: Lucy Roslyn

Designed and typeset by Nick Hern Books, London
Printed in Great Britain by Mimeo Ltd, Huntingdon, Cambridgeshire PE29 6XX

A CIP catalogue record for this book is available from the British Library

ISBN 978 1 83904 097 9

www.nickhernbooks.co.uk

facebook.com/nickhernbooks

twitter.com/nickhernbooks